When I Was Little
Like You

by

Jane Porett

Illustrated by

S. Dmitri Lipczenko

Child Welfare League of America • Washington, DC

Hi, my name is Elizabeth. I'm a grown-up now, but once I was little, like you.

Sometimes when you are little, things happen to you and you don't know what to do. I know, because when I was little, like you, things happened to me. The things that happened to me made me sad and lonely. They made me feel bad about myself.

What I want to tell you about has to do with touching. Some kinds of touches, like hugs, tickles, cuddles, and good-night kisses, usually make you feel good.

But when someone wants to touch or do things to your private parts, or wants you to touch their private parts, it can make you feel bad or scared.

Your private parts are those parts of you that are covered by your swimsuit.

This can happen to either boys or girls. The person who does these things may be an older boy or girl, a man, or a woman. It may be someone you love, like a daddy, a mommy, an aunt, a brother, a baby-sitter, or a friend of the family.

Even though you have always been told to listen to grown-ups, it is okay to say "NO" if it makes you feel bad. Sometimes, though, even if you say "NO," the person won't stop.

When I was little, sometimes my daddy and mommy went out and a friend of theirs took care of me. He touched my private parts and made me touch his. I said, "Please don't," but that didn't stop him.

I know that even worse things happen to other children.

Besides saying no, do you know what else I did? NOTHING! Now that I'm a grown-up, I know that when I was little, like you, I could have done more.

I SHOULD HAVE TOLD SOMEONE
WHAT WAS HAPPENING TO ME!

The person making you feel bad might be someone you love. They might tell you, "It's our secret," or "If you tell, we'll get in trouble." Don't believe them.

Your body belongs to you, and you have the right to decide what happens to it.

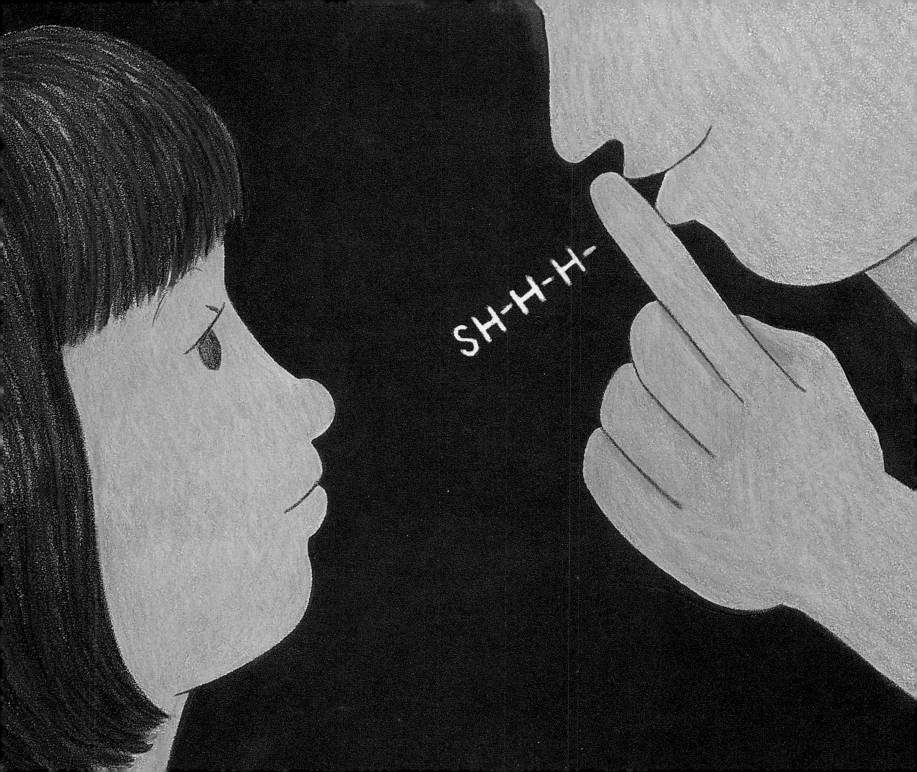

Sometimes this touching can make you feel good, or even special, for a while, but it can also hurt and feel wrong.

Always remember, IT IS NOT YOUR FAULT if this happens to you!

THE ONLY WAY TO MAKE THE PERSON STOP
IS TO TELL A GROWN-UP ABOUT IT.

If the first grown-up you tell doesn't believe you,
keep telling people until someone listens. You can tell
your mom or dad, an aunt, a neighbor, a teacher,
friend, or police officer.

Can you think of anyone else who might listen to you?

The grown-up who does things that hurt your body needs special help called *counseling*.

I know you may think it is easier to pretend the touching didn't happen to you, or even to make up imaginary friends it happened to instead of you.

Telling someone may be one of the hardest things you ever have to do. But after you find someone who can help you, you don't have to be scared or hurt anymore.

If someone you know has a problem like mine, help them find a grown-up to tell. Be sure your friend knows that they didn't do anything wrong.

I'm glad I told you what happened to me when I was little. I hope that my story will help you tell someone if something like this happens to you.

About the Author

When I Was Little Like You is based on the childhood experiences of Jane Porett, who was not able to confront her abuser until she was an adult. Wanting to do something positive to help other abused children, she turned her anger into constructive energy and wrote this book.

Porett, a mother of two, has worked for much of her life with children, first as a volunteer with autistic preschoolers and later as an assistant teacher for autistic children and those with pervasive developmental disorders. She credits the support of her husband and family with helping her to come to terms with her past and to acknowledge how it has affected her life today.

About the Illustrator

S. Dmitri Lipczenko is Art Director for the Child Welfare League of America. She received her BFA in design from Carnegie Mellon University and has worked as a designer and an illustrator. This is her first book for children.

© 1993 by the Child Welfare League of America, Inc.

CHILD WELFARE LEAGUE OF AMERICA, INC.
440 First Street, NW, Suite 310, Washington, DC 20001-2085

CURRENT PRINTING (last digit)
10 9 8 7 6 5 4 3 2 1

Book design by S. Dmitri Lipczenko
Printed in Mexico

Library of Congress Cataloging-in-Publication Data
Porett, Jane
      When I was little like you / by Jane Porett ; illustrated by Susan Dmitri Lipczenko.
         p.   cm.
      Summary: The narrator tells children how to recognize sexual abuse and know what to do if it happens to them.
      ISBN 0-87868-530-8: $12.95
      1. Child molesting—Juvenile literature.   2. Child molesting—Prevention—Juvenile Literature.   [1. Child molesting.]
   I. Lipczenko, Susan Dmitri, ill. II. Title.
HV6570.P67   1993
362.7 ' 6—dc20
[E]   93-13974